HOW DO YOU SEE YOURSELF

THE ROAD TO SELF-DISCOVERY

ANTOINE L. SMITH, SR.
FOREWORD: DR. ANTOINETTE HARRELL

How Do You See Yourself? A Guide to Self-Discovery
BY ANTOINE L SMITH SR
Foreword by Antoinette Harrell

Copyright (c) 2025 Antoine L Smith Sr

All rights reserved. No part of this book may be reproduced in any form or by any means without the written consent of the publisher or author, excepting brief quotes used in reviews and certain other non-commercial uses permitted by copyright law. Published in Independence, Louisiana, as part of the Jozef Syndicate imprint.

ISBN 978-1-944155-47-6
Library of Congress Control Number: 2025916144
First published in the United States of America

TABLE OF CONTENTS

Foreword 5

Prologue 7

How Do You See Yourself? 12

So As A Man Thinketh 24

Self Inventory 38

Looking Beyond Barriers 49

Power of Life and Death is in the Tongue 61

The Giants in Your Life 71

It Takes Patience and Faith to Achieve Your Goals 86

FOREWORD

In this book, you will learn about yourself and how to face the challenges that have been blocking you from becoming the best version of yourself. Self-discovery sometimes requires some guidance. It is very common for people from all walks of life to face challenges and not know how to seek help. Reading this book is the first step toward self-discovery. This book attempts to help you see yourself. What you think about yourself is more important than what others think about you. You will discover important key points about yourself through each chapter. This journey of self-discovery will empower you to overcome obstacles, build resilience, and embrace your true potential. By understanding your strengths and weaknesses, you can create a roadmap for personal growth and fulfillment. Remember, the path to becoming your best self begins with a single step—choosing to invest in yourself.

We often define ourselves by what others think of us rather than by what we think of ourselves. Self-validation should be the only thing needed. The importance of having a positive support system cannot be overstated. It is, however, your beliefs and knowledge about yourself that should serve as your true foundation. Self-validation will empower you to trust your instincts and make decisions with confidence. Use this book as a GPS to identify obstacles that are holding you back. In every chapter, you will find Bible verses that will help you become the person God intended you to be.

"These verses offer wisdom and encouragement, helping you reflect on your values and align your actions with spiritual teachings. They help to provide comfort in times of doubt and serve as a reminder of the strength and resilience you possess. Meditating on these scriptures will help nurture a deeper understanding of yourself and your purpose. "As you engage with this book, I hope that you will gain significant self-insight. It is my aspiration that you will find it beneficial and enriching."

Dr. Antoinette Harrell

PROLOGUE

Have you ever look in the mirror and ask yourself, "Who am I?" Are you who you say you are? Do you really know, or do you know what was told to you about you. In the journey of self-discovery and self-acceptance, we often find that the answer to the question "Just "who am I? is not a fixed and static identity. It is a continuous process of exploration, reflection, and growth, where we unravel layers of conditioning, societal expectations, and external influences to uncover our authentic selves. Through introspection, self-reflection, and embracing our unique experiences and perspectives, we begin to see ourselves more clearly and confidently define our own identity.

My personal relationship with God (Higher Power) helped me to see myself. My spiritual upbringings and biblical teachings allowed me to grasps how I see myself. It give you strength and hope. I was able to apply the scriptures to my personal life. For example one of my favorite scriptures is: Joshua Chapter 1, verse 5, As I was with Moses, so I will be with thee. That's what I believed and I lived by that everyday of my life. He promised in his word, I know that God is always in control. Those words became my comforter. Do not get me wrong I fall short like everyone else, I find my mind wandering at times and I remind myself to controls my thoughts. Over the years, I learned to write my daily task down on paper. I find that writing down my task helps me to stay focus. I'm still working on developing a closer relationship with God sixty-plus years later.

During one of my son's soccer games, I watched him watched double and triple teams play against my son. Despite all odds against him, he never gave up. It was clear to me that my son was determined. The goal line was a goal he was determined to reach. In his mind, he saw himself as a winner. In life, he applied that same practice to become unstoppable. College was his next step, and he became a successful businessman. How you see yourself is the beginning of everything. For example, if a person sees themselves as incompetent and unworthy, they may lack the confidence to pursue their goals and settle for mediocrity. On the other hand, if someone sees themselves as capable and deserving of success, they are more likely to take risks, work hard, and achieve their aspirations. Self-perception plays a crucial role in shaping our mindset and determining our trajectory in life.

My father died when I was six years old. After my father died, my mother became the head of the household and the breadwinner. When my father was alive, my mother was a true housewife, never worked outside the home. He dedicated every aspect of his life to providing for his family. I wanted to be like my dad and help take care of my mother after he died. I imagined myself helping my mother. To help my mother, I found little odd jobs and gave her the money. Nevertheless, she used it to buy my school clothes. According to her, that helped her. Wanting to be like my dad was not just about the practical aspects of providing financial support. It was also about trying to fill the void he left behind and honor his memory by stepping into his role as a caregiver and provider for my family.

I want to share my personal experience I carefully example three things; the past, present, and future. From this reflection, I applied the insights gained by using the past to learn from my mistakes, the present to make the most of the opportunities in front of me, and the future to set goals and envision the life I want to create for myself. By combining these three perspectives, I was able to make decisions and navigate my personal journey with clarity and purpose. As well as staying focus.

The purpose of this book is to help the reader take a closer look at themselves. The era of your life you want to revisit can be worked on. Where do you want to see yourself in the future? It's time for you to decide what to do. It is time for you to change how you think about yourself. The Bible was my blueprint and manual for navigating my life. My key to success was following the instructions. I used the parables as a GPS to guide my decisions and footsteps. Although I fell from time to time. It was necessary for me to examine myself and recognize my own shortcoming. The Bible can be used as a blueprint for personal growth because it provides guidance, wisdom, and moral teachings that can help individual navigate their lives. By studying the parables and following the instructions found in the Bible, I gained insights into how to make better decisions, overcome shortcomings, and ultimately transform me into the person I aspire to be. I hope this book help you find the pathway. *Psalms 119: Verse 105, Your word is a lamp to my feet and light unto my path.* I wholeheartedly believed this my entire life My goal is to see you achieve your goals. Each chapter should be read and the questions at the end of each chapter should be answered honestly. You should secure your book like you would a diary if you do not want others to see it. You're embarking on a journey of self-discovery, self-help, and self-improvement. Self-discovery allows you to gain a deeper understanding of your values, passions, and strengths. It helps you make more informed decisions and set realistic goals that align with your true self.

The Scriptures in each chapter nurture your spirit and inspire you to reach your full potential. Set aside a few minutes each day to reflect and meditate on the passages. Keep a journal to record thoughts or insights as you apply these teachings to your daily challenges. Discussing these passages with a community group or a friend can offer fresh perspectives and deepen your understanding.

You will learn about yourself through every chapter of this book to achieve your goals. If we all stop and take inventory of our spiritual life, financial life, mental and physical awareness, what will we find? We may discover areas where we excel and areas that need improvement, allowing us to set more realistic and meaningful goals. Your first step toward improving yourself has already been taken by reading this book. To see personal growth, you should read all six chapters and honestly answer the questions at the end of each chapter. Let's get started on a journey of self-discovery and self-improvement. Get yourself a delicious cup of coffee or tea, relax, and start writing as if you are writing in your journal.

1

HOW DO YOU SEE YOURSELF?

*And we were in our own sight as Grasshoppers.
And so we were in their sight.*

Numbers 13:33

While preparing for morning meditation, I brewed a fresh pot of coffee as part of my morning routine. To study my Bible, I grabbed a pencil and notepad and looked up a verse our pastor taught in our Sunday School lesson. He talked about how the spies who was exploring the land of Canaan saw themselves. Number 13:33.

"We saw the giants (Nephilim) the descendants of Anak came from the Nephilim. *We seem as grasshoppers in our own eyes, and we look the same to them."* Number 13:33. For a few minutes, I let that plunder in my mind. "What can I learn from this scripture?"

They appeared as grasshoppers in their own minds as they stood before the giants. The meaning of this verse opened up my mind and thoughts. In spite of the fact that no one told them they were grasshoppers, they told themselves that they were. How do you see yourself? We all have highs and lows in our lives and we can doubt ourselves at times. Sometimes we focus on our weaknesses instead of our strengths. The truth is, we're capable of overcoming any challenge if we believe in ourselves. We must learn to see ourselves as God sees us as strong, capable, and loved." How do you see yourself? That is a question that only you can answer.

I would like to share a part of my life journey. When I was a very young child, my father died, leaving my mother to care for me and my siblings. I dreamed of getting a job to help my mother. I got my first job when I was twelve years old. When I started earning money, I began dreaming of all the things I could do with it. I wanted to purchase my own school clothes to help my mother out. This was during the time you could place an order from Sears & Roebuck Catalog. I couldn't wait until the postman delivered my package. I visualized myself in those new jeans, shirts, and shoes. It was at that moment that I realized I was capable of achieving anything if I put my mind to it. I was able to meet the many challenges of self-discovery, thanks to how I saw myself back then.

It was impossible for anyone to convince me that I couldn't achieve my goals or stop me from becoming the person I wanted to be. At this point, I realized that what others thought of me negatively wouldn't affect my life. I realized that my success depended on my own efforts and determination. No one could define my worth or limit my potential. What I'm saying here is to not let others' negative opinions and fears determine your future. It's very important how you see yourself.

In Psalms 139:14, *"I praise you, for I am fearfully and wonderfully made."* What God is telling us is that he made a special masterpiece when he made each of us. If you do not believe that you are wonderfully made, what causes you to feel this way? It may be a childhood trauma or something terrible that happened to you, leaving you feeling stuck. This was the moment you defined what you thought and felt about yourself. My wife once told me with tears streaming down her cheeks that loneliness led her to God. Although she grew up in a large family, thirteen siblings and parents. She still felt lonely even when surrounded by her family. She said this was where she met God, in her loneliness. She explained how God was there for her at that crucial time. Early on, my wife stressed that she was created for greatness.

Did something in your past give you a negative or positive impression of yourself? It is possible to hear something negative, such as "you will never be successful," or to have been inspired by someone to achieve your dreams. Either way, both can impact a person's life and determine how they view themselves in the future.

Do you ever look in the mirror and think about a new hairstyle or something to spice up your appearance? You decide to make an appointment with your hairstylist or barber. When you sit in the chair, you let them know you want a total makeover, and they immediately get started on a new hairstyle. Let's talk about the inside, in order to have change on the inside you have to start with a changed mind. What does this mean? How do you view and handle situation that arise in your life? Until there is a change with your thought patterns, nothing will change. I stated that I would be very transparent about my journey in my book. I'm keeping that promise by sharing my experiences with you.

I learned that I was overwhelmed and all over the place. Accomplishing my task was difficult. Eventually causing me to lose new business prospects due to what they would say—to many irons in the fire. Changing that old habit became a priority for me. I learned to write things down on my to do list. I started to see how writing things down help me to become more organized and focused. That help me improve my life a great deal.

"What do you want to improve in your life, and how will you achieve it? In my experience, the first step is acknowledging that something is wrong—whether it's self-inflicted or beyond your control. You must stop letting it hinder your progress and prevent you from becoming the person you want to be. If it's something you're doing or have done, this is where accountability becomes essential. Accepting responsibility is key if you truly want to create change."

For example, if you're always running late and somehow just lose track of time, you want to get better at being on time. Running late stresses you. By the time you get to where you are going, you have anxiety. Now, what can you do to avoid this? Try getting up thirty minutes earlier. You can prepare the night or day before. Set your alarm to leave on time." You soon start to see yourself as person you want to become. That is being a person who is always on time.

"One thing that has been very helpful to me is my morning meditation on who I am constantly striving to become. It takes practice to become who you want to be. I found that taking inventory of my personal life was extremely helpful. Taking inventory involved my spiritual life, financial life, relationships, and mental and physical health." Self-reflection can allow you to identify your strengths and weaknesses, providing a clear path for your personal development.

Keep in mind that some things you do are correct and don't need to be changed. However, there is always room for improvement. You should find ways to consistently enhance your skills and knowledge. This can help you unlock new opportunities and achieve greater success in your life. Growth in all areas of our lives are important. How you see yourself and how you see yourself in the future is important. Take note of your steps you're taking to get there.

The habits we form during childhood can be either good or bad. The habits we inherit from our parents can set the foundation for our future and lead us to destinations we want or don't want. Some family habits should be broken. Let me give an example, some family can't manage their finances and their children are developing the same habits. With some imagination you know where this can lead. Other families have get finance habits and they taught their children the importance of managing the money.

After our father passed away, all my siblings got jobs to support our family. I was inspired to do the same and have been working ever since. I learned the value of hard work and the importance of contributing to the well-being of those I care about.

This foundation has driven me to consistently strive for excellence in all my endeavors. A few of my older siblings started drinking and I watched them and didn't want to follow suit.

Although I could easily have taken a drink. The sight of my brother being drunk made me want to stay away from drinking. The thought of becoming an alcoholic was not appealing to me. My mental picture of what it would do to me wasn't what I desired. When one of my brothers started drinking, he would get loud and fight everyone in the house, and I didn't want to do the same. It really discourages me from drinking. In other words, I didn't want to become like my siblings who were drinkers.

One day during Sunday School we were studying how important it is to have a relationship with God and the benefits we get from developing a relationship with him. The preacher pointed out that it take time and it is a process. What he was taught us, is no matter what you're working on it takes time. I want to make this point very clear, you have to stay focus.

My personal relationship with God helped me to overcome negative situations, thoughts and perceptions of myself. Without him I would not have not been able to accomplish my goals and I would have allowed other opinions of me to define me. This is the point I'm pointing out to you, if you do not have a relationship with God, you should consider developing one. What I'm saying to you is God's words serve as a blueprint for my life. One of my favorite bible scriptures is- *I can do all things through Christ who strengthen me; Philippians 4:13*. It let me know that any situation that happened in my life, I had the power to overcome it.

Everything starts with how you see yourself, The way you see yourself is the beginning of everything, it can shapes your beliefs, choices, and actions. A positive self-image can lead to confident decision-making and a willingness to take risks, while a negative self-image may result in hesitation and self-doubt. Ultimately, how you perceive yourself influences the path you choose and the success you achieve.

You can be positively or negatively influenced by people in your circle. Because of this, it is important to choose the right people to surround yourself with. Look for signs such as consistent negativity, manipulation, or lack of support in your interactions with them. Pay attention to how you feel after spending time with them; if you feel drained or anxious, it may be a sign of a toxic relationship. Trust your instincts and consider whether these relationships contribute positively to your personal growth and well-being.

"Two scenarios: one child was told they'd never succeed, and they grew up believing it. Another child was told they could achieve anything and never doubted themselves." The first child may have struggled with self-esteem and faced numerous setbacks, potentially limiting their opportunities and achievements. In contrast, the second child likely pursued their goals with confidence and resilience, leading to a more fulfilling and successful life. This illustrates the powerful impact of positive versus negative reinforcement on an individual's development and future.

Depending on how you view yourself, you may have to peel layers upon layers. Self-discovery is a journey that involves introspection and reflection on your thoughts, beliefs, and values. It requires a willingness to confront uncomfortable truths and embrace change as you uncover different aspects of your identity. Through this process, you gain a deeper understanding of who you are and what truly matters to you.

Explore the next chapters to uncover deeper insights and continue your journey of self-discovery. No one knows you better than you do. It's time to be completely honest with yourself. Gaining a deeper understanding of yourself can lead to improved decision-making and increased self-confidence. By recognizing your strengths and weaknesses, you can navigate life's challenges more effectively.

QUESTIONS

1. How do you see yourself?

   _____

   _____

   _____

2. Do. you have negative thoughts about yourself?

   _____

   _____

   _____

3. Does others negative thoughts affect you? Is so, how?

   _____

   _____

   _____

4. How do you deal with negative thoughts about yourself?

   _____

   _____

   _____

5. What are you willing to do to change it?

_____

_____

_____

2

SO AS A MAN THINKETH

For as a man Thinketh in his heart, So is He.

Proverbs 23:7

For as a man Thinketh in his heart, so is he." A person's thoughts and mindset directly shapes their character. That is why our parents told us to be careful of the company that we keep because of their influence in our life. The way you think signifies, and impacts who you are and what you experience in life. This verse is used to warn against association with people who are inwardly not sincere as their true nature will eventually be revealed by their thoughts and their actions. A wider look at the interpretation beyond the biblical content "As a man Thinketh, so is he" is often used to emphasize the power of positive thinking and the idea that by consciously managing your thoughts you can influence your life outcome. Philippians 4:8, it tells us, *"Finally, brother, whatsoever things are true, whatsoever things are honest, whatsoever things are just, whatsoever things are pure, whatsoever things are lovely, whatsoever things are of good report—if there be any virtue, if there be any praise—think on these things."* And it tells us that in this letter the Apostle Paul was encouraging the Philippian christians to stay focused on what is good and praiseworthy and to put it into practice what you have learned from him.

These proverbs were compiled to teach wisdom, encourage faith in God, and provide practical guidance for living. This refers to your inward calculations which highlight a disconnect between his outward actions and inner thoughts.

"Your thoughts, your associations, and what you do every day have a direct effect on the way you live your life. When you think positively, your outlook on life is positive. Negative thinking leads to negative thoughts, negative direction, negative actions. Therefore, a man is what he thinks. Thoughts can significantly influence our emotions by shaping how we perceive and react to situations. Positive thoughts often lead to feelings of happiness and contentment, while negative thoughts can result in feelings of sadness, and anxiety, or anger. By consciously managing our thoughts, we can better regulate our emotional responses and improve our overall well-being."

This book encourages positive thinking, suggesting that good things will follow. A practical way to practice this is by starting a gratitude journal, where you record things you are thankful for each day. Another method involves reframing negative thoughts by identifying a positive aspect or lesson in difficult situations. Also, surrounding yourself with positive influences, such as supportive friends or uplifting content, can help reinforce an optimistic mindset.

You should limit yourself with social media that speak negative things and news broadcast. Exposing yourself to negative content on social media can significantly impact your mental health. It can lead to increased feelings of anxiety, depression, and low self-esteem as you internalize the negativity. Limiting your exposure to such content can help maintain a more positive mindset and improve overall well-being.

Before I start my day. My first act of the day is prayer. I've heard other motivational speakers say the same thing. Yes I'm reading another author's book on the topic I'm writing about. There is no difference between the two books, they both are basically saying the same things. Prayer should be the first thing you do in the morning. If you haven't learned to start your day off with prayer. Perhaps that is something you should seriously consider. Before you look at your phone, or turn on your television, and see the negativity of the day. It might be a wise idea to rethink how you allow early morning interruptions to intrude into your spirit."

How does one control their negative thoughts? What is the best way to control negative thoughts? One effective technique is practicing mindfulness meditation, which helps you become aware of your thoughts and detach from negative patterns. Cognitive-behavioral techniques, such as challenging and reframing negative thoughts, can also be beneficial. What you think, adventurually manifest itself in your actions. Self transformation starts in your thoughts. We all have subconscious and conscious thoughts. Let me point out there is a difference in subconscious thoughts and conscious thoughts.

Under the conscious mind are mental processes that exist in the subconscious. The conscious mind is responsible for our active thoughts and awareness, while the subconscious mind stores memories, beliefs, and emotions that influence our behaviors and decisions. These two layers of the mind interact continuously, with the subconscious often guiding automatic responses and habits that the conscious mind might not be fully aware of. By becoming more attuned to this interaction, individuals can gain greater control over their actions and reactions, leading to personal growth and improved mental well-being.

Your subconscious mind is like a computer chip, it stores information. Let's talk about this for a minute. If you think you are a failure, you have store this thought in your mind. You have to find a way to delete the negative thoughts before they come to your conscious mind. Let me give an example. Music influence the minds of your young people all over world. Music sets the tone for moods, behaviors and action. If the lyrics are negatives, it can have a negative affect on millions of minds globally. Negative music has cause many youth to act the lyrics and throw their life away based on negative music provoking negative and unwanted action.

Therefore, we must be conscious of what we allow to enter our subconscious mind. Practiced mindfulness and meditation can also help us maintain control of our thoughts. By engaging in activities that promote mental well-being, like reading uplifting books or listening to inspiring music, you can fortify your subconscious against harmful intrusions.

If you consider yourself a failure, you are. When you think you're a winner, that's what you are. So a Man Thinketh, Now, don't get me wrong, I'm not calling you a failure. I'm only speaking about what negative thoughts about yourself can do to you. Many successful people have struggled with self-doubt but have learned to overcome it. For example, the Wright Bros faced numerous setbacks when flying an airplane. They crashed many airplanes before they got off the ground, they never gave up. In other words they believe in their vision.

You have to train your mind and thoughts. Don't get me wrong, but in my line of work as a electrician, I have to stay focused. I worked as a lineman for Entergy Louisiana, LLC., for 36 years. I had to clear somethings out of my head to get to work because one mistake, it could have been fatal. So I had to control myself. Some personal issues that were going on in my life, I had to subdue them. Don't get me wrong, every day wasn't sunshine

I had to stay focused to get the job done, and I had to train my thoughts to do so, to where I could perform my duties and not injure myself and co-workers.

I find my relationship with God help me to reflect on my life and thoughts. The power of thoughts influence your character and behavior. Also your personal and professional life. Your thoughts define your character. Earlier in the chapter, I discussed the power and influence of music. What I'm saying here is your thoughts will impact your life.

This chapter was critical for me to write for readers to understand the power of "So A Man Thinketh." Negative thoughts will cause a negative reaction and an unwanted problem. Positive thinking will improve your life.

My relationship with God, influenced my character. Going back to my childhood where I learned the importance of having a relationship with God. I was taught that I had to carry myself a certain way. My parents also taught me to be careful about who I kept company with so I would not be influenced by negative thinking individuals. Have you ever heard someone say, "If it wasn't for bad luck, I wouldn't have any luck at all?" I know I have. Let's take a moment to plunder this. Because they have repeated this to themselves over and over again, they really start to believe it. If anything happens to them, they'll say, "Ok, there it is." It's like bad luck follows me everywhere. To break the cycle of negative thinking, one can start by practicing gratitude and focusing on the positive aspects of their life. Engaging in mindfulness exercises, such as meditation or journaling, can also help in gaining a clearer perspective and reducing negative thoughts. Surrounding oneself with positive thinking people.

Whenever I wake up, I get a cup of coffee, get ready, and take out my writing pad. My day is planned out according to what I will do for the day. I watch the sun come up while praying and giving thanks to God for allowing me to see another day. In my daily life, I am guided by my thoughts and meditation. It helps me to control my thoughts and keep them from wandering all over the place. Here's an example, if you're thinking negatively about a situation and you spoken negatively about the situation, you're saying it won't work. Positive thinking, on the other hand, can open up possibilities and inspire creative solutions. By maintaining an optimistic outlook, you encourage a mindset that is open to opportunities and resilient in the face of challenges. This mental shift can lead to improved problem-solving abilities and a greater sense of well-being.

This book is written to help you learn that having a relationship with God is essential for positive thinking. We can't handle things and situation on our own. This book is to help you see how important God is in your life. No one can do it all on their own, we all need help. Let me share something with you. My life without God will be terrible. I couldn't even imagine where I would be if it wasn't for him. Perhaps you have tried everything, have you thought about giving God a try?

Come on, what do you have to lose by learning God's way. I can tell you what I had to lose, I have my soul to lose, peace, joy, happiness, and love. I have to much too lose and I'm not going to take that chance.

In Philippians 4:8 *he tells us to think on things that are true. Think on things that are honest, just, what so ever things are lovely.* I'm not saying that things will not happen to you that is out of your control. There is always something to get out of the experience. So we're not dwelling on really the situation that we were in,

It clear that you must think on what you're trying to accomplish, and spend time and effort to make it happen. You're trying to do a positive thing in your life. Trust me on this one, you will see further down the road what will happen for you when you change the company or habit that could be hindering you.

These days we have the internet and you can google anything. If you want to achieve anything you can learn more about the subject online. There is more information then ever before because of the Internet. If you meditate and concentrate on positive thinking and apply yourself, you can achieve your goal.

For example if a little boy dreamed of being a firefighter when he become an adult. Being a firefighter was always on his mind. He made a conscious effort to make sure it came to pass. He had to think positive. I know everything didn't go his way during the process, by staying focused and keeping what he had to do, he became a firefighter. It starts in the mind, and then it goes from there. Your inner thoughts are going to be your outer reaction. Whatever you're holding inside, it's going to come out, because my mother told us, what's in a man, eventually will come out of him. My siblings and I were taught that our thoughts dictate as to what we become and do in life.

Just like a gardener watering their garden. A mind has to be nurtured also. We have to go to Bible study, Sunday school... I don't want to just keep it in a religious form, your secular circle has to be a positive thinking circle. They both can teach you some value lessons that's for sure.

Books like this can help you. The chapter about self-inventory, is getting to know yourself. You're going to open up with yourself. It may be the first time you took a look at yourself. It will turn out to be one of best things you can ever do for yourself.

We all go through so much negativity during the day. You turn on the television, from the president down to local news. It's always something, you have to block out negative news sometimes. To much negative and bad news can overwhelm you. The mundane things of life that we go through every day can become a struggle. Getting up every morning and doing the same thing, but by the same token, we manage to do it. You have learn how to block out negative thoughts. You're going to have to get out of the negative thinking patterns. It takes time to train you mind to think differently. After all you thinking problem for most of your life. Now all over of a sudden you're reading a book that is advising you to think differently.

I dreamed of wanting to write a book, so I had to make the time write the book. I know what the end results will be if I follow every step it takes to become a published author. I had to make investment with a professional publishers, editors, book cover designers to get started. I was committed to writing down my key points for my book.

This chapter emphasizes the importance of being aware of where your mind wanders, and what's on your mind. There are some things that are not beneficial for you. Negative or unproductive thoughts can lead to increased stress and anxiety, hindering your ability to focus and make sound decisions. They'd create self-doubt and diminish your confidence, preventing you from pursuing opportunities or taking necessary risks. By being mindful of these thoughts, you can actively work to redirect your mental energy towards more positive and constructive patterns.

The difference between imitate and emulate, which sound similar but are different, was discussed at church. When you imitate someone, you return to yourself, but when you emulate someone, you become that person. Listening to them, and talking like them, then you become mentally, in your mind, reacting the way they do. You're emulating, not imitating, so it's a carbon copy. If it positive that's ok. If negative you need to eliminate it.

Proverbs 23:7, *"For as a man Thinketh in his heart, so is he."* That's very important. Our thoughts shape our character as to who we are. And you can tell when people enjoy being around you, because they know they're getting something positive from you.

It starts with a thought because your belief brings on your behavior. Whatever you believe, that's how you behave. It starts in the mind and then we act it out because what's in us is coming out, because we thought it. That's where it all starts from, in the mind.

QUESTIONS

1. What are your thoughts about yourself?

   _____
   _____
   _____

2. Do you feel good about yourself?

   _____
   _____
   _____

3. What do you want to change about yourself?

   _____
   _____
   _____

4. If you have negatives thoughts, were are they coming from?

   _____
   _____
   _____

5. What habits do you have that can hinder you from moving forward?

_____
_____
_____

3

SELF INVENTORY

I can do all things through Christ who strengthened me.

Philippians 4:13

We all need to do self inventory about our life. Our habits, and daily routines are important. The day to day concerns of life can weigh on us if we do not stop to take inventory. We become unimaginative because we are in a state of tunnel vision. The situations that we face can get us out of focus. I am not saying that the mundane things is a bad thing. I am encouraging you take inventory of your life in every aspect. Aspect of life meaning your spiritual, physical, mental and emotional state.

Self inventory is a process of evaluating your strength, and weakness. Your values and your goals. It can also involve identifying things that you feel resentment toward or hurt by and how you can respond differently to them. God's forgiveness is boundless, it allows individuals to heal from past wounds and start a new, emphasizing that their past or failures never define who your are.

Examining yourself has the benefit of allowing you to look at yourself in the mirror. As you do so, you get to see your true self, you get to examine your past and where you have been. What you have done. Whether it was good or bad, you can reflect on your life. Journaling your thoughts and experiences is an excellent way to practice self-examination. Meditating regularly can help you gain clarity and insight into your emotions and actions. Seeking feedback from trusted friends or mentors can also provide valuable perspectives on your behavior and decisions.

Your life will guide you during your introspection. Introspection is crucial for personal growth as it allows individuals to reflect on their thoughts, feelings, and actions. By understanding oneself better, one can identify areas for improvement and make conscious decisions to enhance their life. This self-awareness leads to more meaningful relationships and a deeper sense of fulfillment.

If you stop and do so, you will look at your mental capacity in life and seeing just where you are mentally. It will let you know the direction that you are heading in life. By taking inventory, you are able to see just where you are by examining your past, present, and your future. It will open your eyes to help you see clearly so you can accomplish your goal.

You want to look at your spiritual, your physical, mental and, your financial aspect. Each one is very important. You may even add other essential things to look at. Many of us have asked this question. What is our purpose in life? Purpose gives you a reason to live, gives you a reason to look forward to, it gives you something to anticipate. It helps to give you a clear vision.. We all have a vision that we are trying to achieve.

Introspection aids in making more informed and thoughtful decisions by allowing you to evaluate your motivations and desires. This process helps in aligning your choices with personal values and long-term goals. Introspective decisions lead to more satisfying and purposeful outcomes.

You need to be totally honest with yourself in this chapter by taking a self-assessment. Being honest you may uncover areas for personal growth and development that you hadn't previously acknowledged. This self-awareness can lead to more targeted efforts to improve and ultimately achieve your goals. It can help you build a clearer understanding of your strengths, which can be leveraged for future success.

It's important that you write these things down so you will know which way to start. It provide you will a clear picture that can help you redirect yourself. Many successful write down their daily task and keep a calendar handy. With electronic phones, you can keep notes and your schedule appointments on our phone. Also, a reminder that can be very helpful. What I'm trying to convey to the you in this the importance of taking self-inventory.

You got to start somewhere. Taking inventory is the first start of seeing where you are at. We all have develop bad habits throughout the years. We all need to break bad habits. Some habits are good, some habits are bad. If a person knows a habit is bad, do you think that doing self-inventory can help them change that? This chapter can help motivate you to change?

Yes, you will have to be totally honest with yourself. That's the only way you're going to be able to see the true you. By doing so, you're opening up with God, with others, and you can see what aspect of life that you need to improve on by being honest with yourself. What is being honest and taking the inventory? As I said, you have all the cards with the face up where you can read them clearly. When you're being truthful with yourself, you can read your life clearly. That way, you can make the right move as to what direction you need to go in.

You can't take inventory unless you're very open and honest. That way, you get to see every aspect. We're not saying everything is bad, but you get to see where you need to improve at. Do you think that people stop to take inventory of themselves? Yes, everybody does. Everybody looks at their past, their present, and their future as to where they're headed. We all do it. I'm encouraging you to stop and do inventory of yourself and evaluate you.

This is a individual decision. By the end of this chapter you should have learn more about yourself then you knew before. When you take self-inventory, now it's time to take accountabilities for your actions and choices. In accountabilities you'll see your strength and weakness. This will let you know what you need to work on in your life. Do you have a willingness to change? In order to improve your development there has to be a change of mind. Philippians 2:5 *Let this mind be in you that was also in Christ Jesus.* Sometimes our strength and abilities are not enough. We have to seek a higher power to get to the next level in our life. There comes a time when we realize that we can't do it by ourselves and it can become overwhelming this is the time to seek the higher power. When you realize that you need some additional help, things can change. When you have done all you can physically, emotionally, and mentally- and see that it is not working at this point you need to seek spiritual guidance. With spiritual guidance. It gives us other options in life. Sometimes we get stuck in old habits and old habits are hard to break. Sometimes the mundanes things in life can distract you, not all the time the mundane things in life is bad. It's what you call life.

By you taking self-inventory, you can learn how to balance the mundane things of life. You may be out of balance. Giving to much attention to one things and not enough to the other. After doing all of this, you need to stop and look at what direction you need to go in. There will always be cross roads and oftentimes we as humans will travel the road of least resistance and basically repeating over and over and expecting a different result. (That is the definition of insanity)

We all know when we're out of balance and out of focus, but the question is, when are we going to take responsibility? You must take responsibility if you want to succeed. You need to address your strengths and weaknesses. It is sometimes difficult to move forward in life when you have failed in the past. It could also be negative opinions others have about you and what they think of you, that have hindered your progress. Are you afraid of the challenges you face everyday? We all face challenges on this planet. Do you fear failure because it has been passed down through generations in your family? Overcoming fear is crucial to personal growth and success. Facing and conquering fears can lead to newfound confidence and resilience, empowering you to pursue your goal. The first area we should be looking at is how we think in our mind. *Philippians 2:5 tells us to let this mind be in you that was also in Christ Jesus.* First, it starts with the mind. When we get our mind straight, we can work on other things in our life. When I say getting your mind straight, It's the way we think, the way we see life, the way we look at things. When we do inventory, we have to change our point of view because sometimes we can be on the wrong path, or associating with the wrong people. This leads us to think we are doing well, but in reality, we're taking ourselves down the wrong path all the time. First, you have to change your mind in order to find out if you're in the right state of mind. It all begins with determination. Embracing challenges as opportunities for learning and development can transform obstacles into stepping stones on your journey. Reflecting on your values and goals can help determine if you're aligned with your true purpose. Seeking feedback from trusted friends or mentors can provide an external perspective on your actions and choices. It will help to pay attention to your emotions and overall satisfaction can indicate whether your current path is fulfilling or requires adjustment.

This book is all about you. What is your connection with God? Yes, that's right I said it, for once in you life here a book that caters to you. Well, this book is all about you. It provides personalized reflections and exercises to help you explore your spiritual beliefs and strengthen your relationship with the divine. Each chapter is designed to guide you on a journey of self-discovery, offering insights and practices tailored to your unique spiritual path. Throughout the pages, you'll find the tools to deepen your faith and connect with God in a meaningful way as you take inventory of yourself and every aspect in your life.

The exercises can be easily incorporated into your daily routine, allowing you to set aside a few moments each day for reflection and meditation. Simple practices such as journaling your thoughts, engaging in mindful prayer, or reading a passage of scripture can help you stay grounded and attuned to your spiritual needs. By consistently dedicating time to these activities, you'll cultivate a deeper, more personal connection with God.

Self-inventory has so much to offer. However, it can be challenging to confront personal weaknesses and limitations. The process requires honesty and self-reflection, which can be uncomfortable for many individuals. This step is essential for growth. This is a very important step that should not be skipped.

My life was analyzed when I took an inventory of all the areas. However, I would like to speak about my business. For my business to be successful, I had to do a few things. To accomplish the goals of obtaining permits and registrations, I had to assess my personal life, finances, and time. By assessing my personal life, I was able to identify any potential distractions or commitments that could interfere with my business goals. This allowed me to allocate my time more effectively and ensure that my energy was focused on building the business. Additionally, understanding my personal strengths and weaknesses helped me make informed decisions and leverage my abilities to drive success.

As I looked at my own spiritual goals, I realized that I wanted a closer relationship with God. It was during a quiet morning walk in nature that I felt an overwhelming sense of peace and connection. The beauty and tranquility of my surroundings made me realize how much I longed for a deeper spiritual understanding. This experience inspired me to seek a more meaningful and personal relationship with God. I always practice taking an inventory of life on a regular basis. This isn't something that can be done one time in your life. It is on going.

QUESTIONS

1. What do you want to take self-inventory of in your life?

   _____
   _____
   _____

2. Have you evaluated your spiritual life?

   _____
   _____
   _____

3. Have you evaluated your personal life?

   _____
   _____
   _____

4. What did you learn about your self-inventory?

   _____
   _____
   _____

5. How can it impact your outcome in your life.

_____

_____

_____

4

LOOKING BEYOND BARRIERS

When she had heard of Jesus came in the press behind, and touched his garment.

Mark 5:27

The definition of insanity is doing the same thing and expecting different results. Since you are trying to improve life, you have to break the habits you are doing. It is about gaining, and having a purpose. To accomplish that, you need to make some changes. You're doing things that aren't conducive to progress. Therefore, it is very important that you identify the habits that are hindering you and make changes because you are trying to gain a purpose, a plan, and goals. With your current mindset, you will not be able to accomplish it. Philippians 2:5 tells us to have the same mind that Christ Jesus had. The change must start with the mind. In order to improve your life habits, you must start by changing the habits you have created.

You will stagnate if you continue to let these habits dominate your life. Creating bad habits can lead to bad consequences. In some cases, these bad habit can be passed down generation to generation. Consequently, it is important to associate with people who think positive, read positive scriptures, and read positive material. Your spiritual well-being is no different from your physical well-being.

You must be completely honest with yourself. You see your habits and the barriers that are holding you back by writing these things down. This will allow you to prioritize those habits. You can fix one if one is more severe than the other. You can address one barrier and alleviate two simply by writing them down, and they don't have to be arranged in any particular order. Acknowledging them, however, is a step forward in changing unproductive habits.

This chapter will help you address different aspects of your life. What does your self-inventory say about you? Each chapter has its own content. You will gain a better understanding of yourself as a result of reading them. It's only when you are honest with yourself that you can see where you stand. Practicing mindfulness can help you become more aware of your thoughts and feelings, which can lead to greater self-honesty. Regularly keeping a journal allows you to reflect on your experiences and recognize patterns in your behavior.

It is for this reason I am writing this book, to help you look beyond your barriers, since I meet a lot of people who do not look beyond theirs. My goal is to get you to see how you can look past your barriers. You need to take control of your life and make the necessary changes to overcome these obstacles. Surround yourself with positive influences and focus on what you can do to improve your situation. Remember, the only thing holding you back is yourself.

Your perspective on things will need to change. To begin with, having a forgiving heart is the first step. Forgiveness is essential. Forgive yourself first, then move on to forgiving others. You may need to forgive yourself for something that happened in your life. There is no better time to do that than now. Forgiveness allows you to release the burden of resentment and anger, freeing up emotional energy to pursue personal growth. It opens the door to healing and self-reflection, enabling you to learn from past experiences and move forward with a renewed sense of purpose.

Benchmarks are essential. It's not enough to say, "I'm going north." You have to know how far north you're going. Benchmarks refer to something to aim for, something to look forward to. In my business, I had to take things step by step. The top wasn't reached just by stepping. To reach the top, I had to make incremental progress. It was necessary for me to set a benchmark. Here is where I had to go first, here is where I had to go second, and here is what I had to do next. As I progressed, I was able to look beyond the barriers because they were behind me at every step. Having a benchmark for where you want to be is very important. When you reach your destination, look again and take one more step forward. The importance of looking beyond barriers cannot be overstated. It is a very important chapter in your life.

My book was inspired by conversations I had with so many people. Everybody has barriers to overcome. It's just the nature of the beast. No matter who you are or where you come from, challenges are an inevitable part of life. Each person faces their own set of obstacles, but finding ways to overcome them is a shared human experience. This journey of perseverance and growth is what connects us all. Some days will be better than others. It's important to focus on the things you can control and practice gratitude by acknowledging the positives in your life. Incorporating mindfulness techniques, such as meditation or deep breathing exercises, can help center your thoughts and reduce stress. Ultimately, it's not how many times you fall, but how many times you get back up that counts.

It is important to understand that a delay is not a denial in the process you're trying to obtain. If you want it to happen on Monday, Tuesday is also fine. Adapt to change with an open mind. Flexibility allows you to adjust to unexpected circumstances and maintain progress toward your goals. Embracing flexibility can reduce stress and improve overall satisfaction in both personal and professional aspects of life.

Don't give up, keep going. In life, we know the old saying: "Don't put off until tomorrow what you can do today." Yes, that's true. Sometimes you have to delay knocking down these barriers until the next day in order to get them down. A delay isn't a denial. This is all part of the process of getting it done. That's what they call the ups and downs of life. Our only option is to deal with them, but we cannot let them keep us down. When you get knocked down ten times, you get up eleven times. It's just a matter of keep moving forward. In order to reach the mark of a high calling, you just need to press forward. Your benchmark is set. It won't stop you from getting there, and you won't let anything stand in your way. In order to break these habits, you need to stay focused.

Writing down both positive and negative habits can help identify priorities and focus on what matters most. Some tasks can be delayed without significant consequences, while others require immediate attention. Documenting these habits can guide decision-making and clarify the path forward. In a previous book, I discussed my approach to writing things down. Establishing a sense of direction is crucial, although the specific order of tasks is less significant. The key is to record them and keep them visible, enabling effective prioritization. This practice is integral to my daily life, as it helps me manage the mental clutter of routine tasks, freeing me from the need to rely on memory

Tracking good and bad habits in daily life helps prioritize changes. The saying 'take the bull by the horns' means facing challenges directly and confidently. By addressing challenges, you can control habits and make positive changes. Overcoming barriers fosters growth, confidence, resilience, and new opportunities for success."This process not only builds character but also enhances decision-making skills. By consistently tackling obstacles, individuals develop a proactive mindset, enabling them to handle future challenges more effectively. You are capable of doing it.

"I've been writing down my thoughts for many years, a habit rooted in childhood memories of my mother leaving handwritten notes on the refrigerator. At the time, I didn't grasp their significance, but as I grew older, I came to appreciate their value. During my years working for Entergy, I developed the practice of jotting down notes at work. It wasn't necessary for me to memorize everything; my pad held all the information I needed, organized after careful review. Yet, the most critical details were always written down. This practice became indispensable, and I encourage you to adopt it as well."

The barriers that have hindered you—the bad habits—can be overcome by following the provided formula. Breaking these habits will help you feel, look, and think better, giving you a more positive outlook on life. The process begins with acknowledging these habits, identifying triggers, setting achievable goals, and creating a step-by-step plan to replace negative habits with positive ones. The formula emphasizes consistency and accountability, enabling you to track your progress and make adjustments as needed. Mindfulness and self-reflection ensure that the changes you make are both sustainable and meaningful. Try it and see what happens.

These habits can entangle you, holding you back like quicksand if you allow them to dominate your life. Left unchecked, they can grow into a destructive force, sapping your energy and potential. Recognizing when a habit no longer serves you is the first step toward transformation. Breaking free demands awareness, unwavering commitment, and often the encouragement of others.

By substituting it with a positive habit, you can cultivate a vibrant, healthier, and more productive lifestyle.

Do what it takes to break the barrier that has been holding you back. It will not be easy. My point is that it is possible if you put your mind to it and work hard at it. There will be times when the road will be difficult and challenging. However, each obstacle you overcome will make you stronger and more resilient. Remember, every step forward, no matter how small, is progress. Stay focused on your goals, and trust in your ability to achieve them.

This brings me to a scripture in the Bible, *I can do all things through Christ who strengthens me. Philippians 4:13*. This verse serves as a powerful reminder that, with faith, individuals can overcome challenges and achieve their goals. It encourages us to trust in our spiritual strengths and resilience. Scripture provides guidance and comfort, offering wisdom and encouragement in times of need. It can serve as a source of inspiration and motivation, helping us to navigate life's ups and downs with a sense of purpose and hope. By reflecting on scriptures, people often find clarity and strength to face daily challenges.

Every chapter describes a different aspect of our lives. What do you think about yourself based on the self-inventory? All of these chapters are available individually. You will see yourself by reading them. Do not be afraid to break barriers. Reading the chapters individually allows you to focus on specific aspects of your life, making it easier to identify areas for improvement. This approach also provides the flexibility to reflect deeply on each topic without feeling overwhelmed by too much information at once. It encourages a more personalized and meaningful journey of self-discovery.

"I want to help you accomplish your goals. I'm also writing from my own experience and using my experiences to help others like you. Remember, success is a journey, not a destination. Stay focused, stay positive, and take one step at a time toward your goals. Believe in yourself and your ability to overcome challenges, and you'll be amazed at what you can achieve."You have the power to create the life you desire, and every small step you take brings you closer to your dreams. Embrace the process, learn from your experiences, and never stop striving for progress. With determination and perseverance, you can achieve greatness and inspire others along the way.

At the end of each chapters the question is designed to help you get to know yourself. These questions often encourage introspection by asking about your values, goals, and personal experiences. They might prompt you to reflect on your strengths and weaknesses, or to consider how past events have shaped your current perspectives. They can facilitate exploration of your dreams and aspirations, guiding you towards a deeper understanding of your identity.

"There comes a time in everyone's life when they break through a barrier. Whether it's on the job or being the first person in their family to earn a degree, that individual is determined to achieve their goal.

The sense of accomplishment is overwhelming, and a wave of pride washes over them as they realize the magnitude of their achievement. Relief and joy intermingle, knowing that their hard work and perseverance have finally paid off. This triumph often instills a renewed sense of confidence and motivation to tackle future challenges. Now, let that person be you."

QUESTIONS

1. What are your barriers?

   _____
   _____
   _____

2. How are you facing your barriers?

   _____
   _____
   _____

3. Are you looking beyond your barriers?

   _____
   _____
   _____

4. How does your barriers affect your life?

   _____
   _____
   _____

5. Are you afraid to face your barriers?

_____

_____

_____

5

POWER OF LIFE AND DEATH IS IN THE TONGUE

Death and Life are in the Power of the Tongue

Proverbs: 18:21

Proverbs 18:21 tells us that death and life are in the power of the tongue. There's nothing better in the world than speaking encouragement to a sister or brother or family member and waiting-watching their eyes light up in joy. That means we should be taking everything that we say seriously. That is why we should work to build each other up and speaking positive words. Don Long said in the words of a song, encourage yourself. Sometimes you can get caught up with the mundane things of life that weigh you down, and that is when you need the word of God in your heart to encourage yourself. Put that on your agenda and practice that everyday in your of life. Singer Celine Dion said in a song, think twice before you speak. This means to think twice and speak once. It's human nature to want to respond immediately, but taking a pause between speaking can make all the difference by reflecting on what you want to say and assessing the situation. You can make a more informed decision about what you say and how you say it. Think before you speak can help you to avoid embarrassment. Speaking before you think often leads to saying the wrong things at the wrong time. Consider other people's feelings. It is true; words have power, and it mitigates stress, Intelligent people think before they speak. Then what you say is more persuasive. The wise man resonates his words where as a fool does not know when to stop talking.

This means what you speak over yourself determines how you're going to come out. I'm suggesting that you speak positive words in your everyday vocabulary to remind yourself that you're a winner and not a loser. So we're having a few affirmations here that I use in my life every day. I tell myself every day that I'm the head and not the tail. I tell myself that I'm above and not beneath. I'm the lender and not the borrower. I tell myself whenever I get in situations that things don't go as I planned and waiting for the fruition to come to pass, a delay is not a denial. So I keep those words in my inner spirit. When my back is up against the wall and it look like I'm not in a winning position, I tell myself no weapon formed against me will prosper. These affirmations keep me in a positive attitude, a positive way of thinking in life. After the day is over with and everything and the wins and the losses of the day, I tell myself we're more than conquerors.

All of this keeps me in a positive state of mind. By doing so I'm affirming that I'm victorious not a victim. That's what this does for me every day. I'm suggesting to you that you would get some words in your daily vocabulary that will uplift you, inspire you, give you admiration, give you the desire to move forward. So when we say we can't do it, we're speaking down on ourselves, and not telling ourself that can we accomplish anything.

It's very important that we do so because it determines our outlook in life: how high you go, your aptitude in life, and your belief, your behavior, all this works together. Speaking positive, being around positive thinking people you can have a change of mind. People that will motivate you, people that will uplift you, people that will inspire you. I want to throw in a little nugget to you. It doesn't have to be your immediate family. It could be a good friend, a good co-worker, church member. Just choose good company. Someone that's not a relative of yours, but you're are inspired by them, that all that really matter in the end.

I'm very conscious of the company I keep and who I surround myself with. We all need to be with people who are not just hearers of the word, but are doers of the word. They will help you in your personal life because what they are saying and doing is inspiring you..

Some people will inspiring you to become your best self and motivate you to achieve your goals. I want to be like him, I want to be like her. We hear that all the time. When I was a kid growing up, I really admire Bishop Joe Dalton because he was hard working and honest man. He lived in my neighborhood and became a mentor for me after my father passed. I really looked up to him. He had my best interest at heart. We needed each other.

The words you speak to yourself can help you in your own personal life. It is very important that you do not speak negative, that you speak positive over your life and the life of your family One thing that we really take for granted is the music that we listen to. Those words carry lots of weight, those words have a bearing on our lives, on your life. It's important that you listen to positive lyrics and music that have a positive outcome on your life.

Let's use music with negativity in it. A lot of times the music today's youth listen to, some try to act it out. You hear negative music, you're acting out that negative side, you're going to get a negative result. So many youth have died, in prison or got hurt because of the music they listen to.. We listen to positive music.

Some people quote positive scriptures. They'd say positive things to themselves. When we practice what we preach to ourselves, we can spread it among others. That is why I'm encouraging you to speak positive to because life and death is in the power of the tongue. So I would encourage you to get your scripture for every day to keep in your heart when things are not going right in life. For me, it's Joshua, the first chapter. *God told Joshua as I was with Moses, I'll be with you also, I'll never fail thee nor forsake thee.* He inspired Joshua to be of good courage, be of a good cheer. I'm inspiring you to do the same thing.

With that, as you get older, you meet different people. Everybody is not negative thinking. You need to graph some of what those people have been telling you in life because they're trying to encourage you. It might be a teacher at school that told you something and it gravitated with you and you start applying it to your everyday life. So, yes, we do hear some positive things, but as some people have said inspire us, we need to gravitate to those people.

When you attend church and hear things that the preacher said during Sunday school lesson or bible study, that inspires you, that gives you hope. Let this chapter inspire you. Hope is a powerful word. That word can really keep a person alive because they're hoping that it's going to change. So, I would encourage you to get with somebody that has an encourage spirit, and encouraging attitude.

The first thing we can recognize when life and death is in the power of the tongue, you can hear the words that you say, what effect they have on you. The words that have an negative effect, you feel that. Then you speak calm and positive words, you see the reaction. You notice how you feel.

A subconscious mind is your deep thoughts and what you're saying about yourself will determine how you come out in life. So, it's very important that we be careful as to what we say about ourselves. We have to speak positive words upon ourselves. Then we can pass it down to our children and other family members. Everybody see you always upbeat. They seem to be getting what they want in life. In order for them to do that, they had to have a change of mind. Start with your mind first, and then you can work on the rest later. One step at a time. Life is a marathon. Life is not a sprint. It's not an overnight thing. We have to constantly work on ourselves. We have to work on ourselves daily. *Paul made the statement, every time you try to do good, evil is present on every hand.* So, therefore, we know the state that we are in, we're in a sinful state. You want to minimize as much as possible the negativity in your life, you will maximize positive result. We shouldn't speak ill of anybody. We've given them positive words in life to change them, too, we know it worked for us. It will work for you, also. You're spreading the good word of faith with people. When they see that, they want to be just like you because somebody is always looking at you. You're giving them a positive outlook on life.

Don't just start blurting out and blabbering off. Small talk can be harmful whether it is intentional or intentional. Like I said earlier, life is a process. You have to work on this. This doesn't come overnight. You've got to be habitual with the change. You just can't do it two days and stop three. It has to become a part of your life. Because if you get with the negative people, you're going to start talking, doing, and saying just what they say. There's got to be a change of your attitude, change of your mind, a change of the way you do things, and a change of the people that you keep company with because they have an impact on how you come out. You're trying to fit in.

Sometimes you might think you're a social misfit, sometimes you might be bullied, sometimes you might think of trying to fit in. But no, that's not the case. You have to get your own identity. It's start with having a positive thinking and a positive attitude. We just have to change our way of doing things. Change some of the people that is in our circle. We talked about that the other day at church, having a positive friendship circle. You know, we all have habits. Some habits you just got to break in order for a change.

You just can't keep doing the same thin and expect a change. The Bible tells us to be slow to anger. Reminding us of think twice and speak once. That's what I'm trying to say. So, we have to be careful. A lot of times you just don't blab out something. You think about what you're going to say because you speaks the words. Remember words have power. Your words can uplift or destroy someone. Sometimes what you say, they don't get over it as quick. So, it's very important that we be mindful of the words that we say.

Others negative opinion of you shouldn't have and impact on our life. My connection with God and how I see myself matter to me the most. That is my strength. What I want you as the reader to understand having a relationship with God can help you face any obstacles. Do not allow other negative thoughts of you influence your life, do not allow what others say about you affect your life.

As God promised in his word, that we're the head and not the tail. You must believe in this, look around and see what he have done for you and what he has brought you through. He is telling us, that he is the one in charge and he can do all things. He tells us to be patient and wait on him. It is not what they call you but what you answer to. Please keep this in mind.

QUESTIONS

1. Are you speaking positive or negative things against self?

   _____
   _____
   _____

2. Did anyone ever speak negatively about you?

   _____
   _____
   _____

3. Did anyone ever speak positive things about you?

   _____
   _____
   _____

4. How did that affect you today?

   _____
   _____
   _____

5. Did you believe the negative things they said?   ?

_____

_____

_____

6

THE GIANTS IN YOUR LIFE

Who is this uncircumcised Philistine that he should defy the armies of the Living God

1 Samuel 17:26

There are giants in your life that you must face. In this chapter, you will learn about your giants. Our life are filled with giants we must face. I'm reminded of a chapter in the Bible when the children of Israel were freed from slavery in Egypt. Egypt was still in them when they left Egypt. The mentality of slavery remained the same. Despite having been set free. Their mentality was still one of slavery. Overcoming these internal giants is crucial for personal growth and transformation. They're often the barriers that prevent us from reaching our full potential and living a fulfilling life. By confronting and defeating these giants, we can break free from limiting beliefs and embrace a mindset of freedom and possibility.

You may face challenges in your life that are giants. No matter how big or small a problem can be, giants are tough to deal with. However, you must always remember that you can defeat the giant. What if we choose to run to God and rely on his strength to help us instead of trying to fix the problem all along. 1 Samuel 17, talks about David victory over the giant. David said in 17:45, " You come against me with the sword, spear, and javelin, but I come against you in the name of the Lord Almighty, the God of the armies of Israel, whom you have defied." We can not only defeat the giants, but the Lord will make us stronger in the process.

Giants come in all different forms and sizes. The giants just keep on coming in our lives. The old saying is, if it ain't one thing, it's something else. When you get over one thing, something else is waiting on you. Giants can be setbacks, pressure, obstacles, and challenges. They can be financial, family matters, health issues or chronic pain, life-threatening disease. They can affect you mentally.

Every experience has a lesson to teach. From personal experience, I can say that every lesson I have learned is valuable. I was able to help others through the lessons I learned. For instance, I gained a great deal of knowledge about writing books and becoming an author. I can now assist someone who wants to write a book but does not know where to begin. In sharing with them, I learned both pros and cons. Do's and don'ts, mistakes and failures. I had to endure working and facing the mundane things of life that could hinder my writing. There was a possibility that it could have been a giant. One of my giants while writing this book was reading the manuscript over and over. It was challenging because just about when I thought I was finished I found somethings that needed to be added and some statement had to be clear up for clarity. For some people, they would have become discouraged. I was to close to the finishing to quit. Quitting wasn't an options. I refuse to let it become a giant.

Hebrew 11:1 "Now faith is the substance of things hoped for, the evidence of things not seen." You must be courageous. Courageous is the willingness to act in obedience to God, even when afraid. It is the mental and moral strength to resist opposition, danger, and hardship. It implies firmness of mind and will in the face of danger or extreme difficulty. We must trust God always. Proverbs 3:5-6 tells us to trust in the Lord with all your heart and lean not to your own understanding. In all your ways acknowledge him, and he shall direct your path.

Your first step in facing your giant is to know whose battle this is. Let me remind you again in 1 Samuel 17:14, David said to Goliath, "All those gathered here will know that it is not by sword or spear that the Lord saves. For the battle is the Lord's, and he will give all of you into our hand." David asks a question, Israel, "For who is this uncircumcised Philistine that he should defy the armies of the living God?" This is how we should approach situation in our life, knowing that God is always in control. He says, here, what are you afraid of. Sometimes the unknown things that we face in life can be a giant because we don't know the outcome of the situation. The unknowns of life is a part of life that is unpredictable and uncertain. It can be scary, but it can also lead to surprise and new possibilities.

Fear, the unknown is a natural response to situation. We don't fully understand. It can be a fundamental human fear, even more important than fear of death. Fear and uncertainty can lead to anxiety, stress, and feeling of powerless. That means that we should turn all these situations over to the Lord, let him handle our battle. Sometimes we want to take actions. If we would let him do it— he promised Abraham a child. Abraham and Sarah said that he was waiting too long. They tried to help God out and went to their handmaid. The child by handmaid wasn't the promise child. The battle that he was facing was a mental battle of him thinking that it's taking God too long. So all he had to do was just wait on the Lord and see what he had in store. This chapter is so important because we all go through battles in life. We all have giants in life. Everybody got something that they're going through. So whether you got one thing, they got something else, it's still a giant, it's a hurdle, it's an obstacle that we have to cross in life.

This chapter will inspire you to confront the giant in your life. Have you access your giant at all? How do you see your giant? One thing about your giant, it isn't hiding, your giant is confronting you. So it's very easy to identify the giant because it's right before you. The things that you're confronted with every day, life itself is a giant.

For example, a person who is battling cancer is facing a real giant. They are facing radiation, and chemo treatments, in some cases it could have taken them two to three years and in the process of healing, it took a lot of determination, that was their giant. That can be a major giant in their life because it's somethings that they're faced with. If you don't have your health and strength, that's a giant. It really doesn't matter how big the other giants in your life are if you do not have your health and strength. Let talk generational giants. Some people may have drugs addiction or gambling habit. The money that they were spending gambling or on drugs their family and future generations was suffering as a result of their addiction. So that giant can be generational. They created this giant. This is somewhat different from just everyday things of life that we can face. With this giant their family's suffers, the children are suffering because the money that they're wasting on this habit could have been put forward in the household.

That creates a bigger giant. This giant that I'm talking about now is a generational giant. He's passing this down. "This isn't just stopping here as television commercial said the buck stops here. This is passed down. "Some maybe fearful of facing their giant. There is a saying "Fear is false evidence appear real." The challenge can be so big that we think we can not overcome it. We think the giant will take us out instead of us overthrowing the giant. But it's very important, and I want to stress this again, you have got to face it before you can fix it. It may seem like it beating down. Or it may set you back. But the issue is, the giant is there to take you out.

David had God with him. What I"m asking in this question, how do you see yourself? Your relationship with God will teach you how to overcome your giants. If you do not have a strong spiritual background, the giant will overthrow you. David picked up about five stones because Goliath had some brothers. In that story, he was talking, if David would not have taken Goliath out, another one was coming. That's what happened in our life. The giants just keep on coming.

He had one stone for each brother, you see. The same biblical word. They work in all situations. But we need to have more than one word in our spirit, more than one verse, so that we can overthrow these giants that keep coming in our life. I strongly recommend that you read Bible scriptures every day.

I draw my daily strength from the 23rd Psalm, The LORD is my Shepherd I shall not want that's where my strength comes from. As I was with Moses, I will be with you also Joshua 1:5. It Because if you don't face it, you can't fix it. So in order to fix what the problem is, we have to face it head on and we have to be honest with ourselves and true. That way we can alleviate the issue that is before us. Even if you don't alleviate it, you can dilute it so to where it would not be a major issue in your life. We have to face the issues, the giants that we confront on an everyday basis.

First, you have to be true with yourself and acknowledge that you have giants in your life. Whether it be a substance abuse or whether anything that can hinder the progress. In the mind is where it all starts. The mundane things of life can be a giant, a challenge of everyday, it's very important that we face it head on.

I've had plenty giants in my life like everyone else. I had to overcome some battles with somethings in my life. Speaking about challenges in life when it came down to my line of work in the electrical field. I had to concentrate on my work because it was a matter of life and death. Every day at work it was a challenge at times for me to remain focus. Things was coming up, the phone was ringing. Paying attention to all the electrical pole around me at all times.

I had to do self-inventory and look back over my life. My spiritual background that I was reared on taught that I can overcome anything. That helped me out a lot in my life. To this day, I used those scriptures and lessons. It plays a very important role in our life, whether we admit it or not. Our spiritual walk, it allows us to face challenge and the hurdles that we have to cross in life. It allows us to know that we can achieve. God let's us know that we are the head and not the tail. We're above and not beneath. We're the lender, not the borrower. All these things that we keep in our spirit lets us know that we can be victorious.

If you don't face your problem or problems head on as David did with the giant Goliath your giant will attack you. David said something the Philistine that were inspirational to me. "David spake to the men that stood by him, saying, What shall be done to the man that killeth this Philistine, and taketh away the reproach from Israel? for who is this uncircumcised Philistine, that he should defy the armies of the living God? David also said this uncircumcised Philistine, he was meaning that he's not a Christian. He's not one of God's chosen people. How is he going to overthrow God's people? That's the way we have to look at our giants in life.

There are somethings you have to take care of right then. Somethings you can't let drag on and you must stay on top of it and get it. Conquering your giant should be an priority otherwise it will overthrow you. Or it will overtake you simply because it needs to be handled right now.

A lot of times we can take on other people's issues. If you are a person that like to help everyone and you're exhausted with their problems. You need to step back and help yourself first. When you take airline flight the first the airline steward tell you to do is put on your own oxygen mask first and then help the next person in event of incident. Sometimes they have to take care of their own because it's a self-inflicted wound that they've created. No matter what you try to do financially, mentally, spiritually trying to help them. If they don't handle it themselves it will weigh on you also.

I see it every day in my own life. How do you see yourself? Your spiritual walk with God determines your attitude as to how far you can go in life to overthrow these giants that we face every day. If you do not know you don't know what your giant are, how can you face it? Faith is very important because you have to have something to believe in. Faith is the unseen. You can't see faith. Having a strong faith base, my religious background and the way we was brought up and things that my mom taught us and some things that we didn't have coming up and she would tell us, God will provide. You need to have faith because you don't see where it's coming from. You don't see no evidence of it being processed because of your faith that keeps you strong and you are willing to wait and see what the outcome, the end is going to be.

Now faith is a substance of things, hope for the evidence of things not seen (Hebrew 11:1).

We saw the evidence of it later because we had the faith to stay strong and to trust in the Lord. I saw her, the things that she did not have, she kept the faith and it all come out at the end, everything came out good. My mother was a faith-based person, of course we saw things coming up after our father died, but God provided for us.

It was things like paying our household bills. I witness firsthand how mother took the challenge. I can ensure you that my mother never allowed our utilities to be disconnected. Although at time things was tough and we didn't fall short getting our school clothes and school supplies for the school term. I saw how my mother took on the challenge of provide for her children. No, she didn't have a credit card. She would put our school supplies and clothes on layaway across the summer. That's how she did it and with her faith, it was the way she did things, but at the end, it all came through.

The scripture quoted in this chapter inspired me to stay focused, to keep the faith and at the end, God will find favor in you by doing so, but you have to keep the faith and not doubt. The scriptures were important part of my foundation. I witness firsthand the power of the Bible scriptures working. Regardless to what I went through during the process, I saw it work at the end and that made my faith grow stronger. What he did for our family was reminder of how powerful he is.

I feel compelled to share this information with others in my walk of life, talking to people, sharing things. People confide in me with a lot of situations in their life and some of it's just casual conversation. One of the biggest things that I'm finding out here is people talking about how hurt they are and how they're being treated.

Everyone has giants in their life and my books are covering all of those giants. This chapter is about giants is to help you see your giant and how to face your giant. Some people are trying to earn money, some people are trying to keep their money, that's a giant. At church we discussed how some people won't leave their house because of their possessions, they don't want nothing stolen. That's a giant. They can't do other things because they're afraid to leave their house thinking their home will be burglarized home. That's a giant.

Neglecting to pay your utilities can cause your utilities to be disconnected if you failed to pay your bills or your car can be repossessed, your home can be repossessed simply because you failed to address the giant that's standing before you. Let me give you an example of what I'm talking about. I noticed one person had money to pay their bill, but they refused to pay the bill and they wanted to hold on to the money because they said the money feels good in their pocket. So they end up getting late fines and late fees. That was a giant that was created by their on doings.

That is a mental giant. In his head or her head, they feel that they need to have X amount of dollars in their pocket in order to sustain them mentally. That's a mental issue and that's a giant, whether they admit it or not. This giant was not going to kill them, but this giant made it harder on some situations in their life Because they wanted to hold to their money and not pay the monthly bill, they created another giant.

I stated earlier, the giants just keep on coming. You have to keep moving, life can be a struggle, life is a battle, life is a fight, and you'll forever be fighting giants in our lives. When you ask the question, how can I minimize my giant? Some giant can be minimize, while other giant can't. The bottomline is to avoid trouble that can be giants and other giants that you have no control, learn to lean on the God for direction on how to deal with those giants.

QUESTIONS

1. Have you identify the giants in your life?

2. What are you doing to elevate the giants in your life?

3. How long have you been dealing with the giants in your life?

4. Are you overwhelmed with your giants?

5. What are you willing to do to eliminate the giants?

_____

_____

_____

7

IT TAKES PATIENCE AND FAITH TO ACHIEVE YOUR GOALS

Lord, I believe; Help Thou Mine Unbelief

Mark 9:24

Well, what really shaped me at an early age, I was an active participants in our church. I've been in the same church for 66 years, I had to participate in church services and activities. I to had to re-recite Bible verses and poems on special holidays. I truly believe this shaped the foundation of beliefs in my life. I attended church revivals, vacation Bible study, and all of that helped mold me to who I am today. Because I had a strong foundation to stand on, and it played a vital part in the way I see life.

The circumstances surrounding my father's death when I was six years old affected me in some ways. My family life was a testament to God's work. There was always food, clothing, and shelter available to us. Based on what we had heard, what we were taught, and what we believed about God, I knew a higher power was at work.

Because of the activities that I was involved in, all of these activities were shaping and molding me, and I'm growing in the process. When you reflect back on your life and look back at where you came from, things that you have experienced, things that you have seen - it tells you that there must be a higher power because some things were beyond your control. You really weren't sure how it was going to work out, but when you look back, God brought you through it.

The fact that I'm alive, my children, and family are still here makes me grateful. Additionally, I have the need to live. Gratitude helps me appreciate the small moments and keeps me grounded even during challenging times. It encourages me to focus on the positive aspects of life and encourages a sense of contentment and joy. This mindset motivates me to engage more deeply with my surroundings and nurture my relationships with God. *Lord I believe help my unbelief.* (Mark 9:24)

Although I strayed from those teachings at times, the *Bible instructs us to train up a child in the way he should go, so that when he is old, he will not depart from it.* Proverb 22:6. As a result of being taught to choose right over wrong, I took full responsibility every time I chose to do wrong. My parents taught me this growing up. These teachings instilled a strong sense of accountability and integrity in me as a child and into my adulthood. They guided me in making moral decisions and taking responsibility for my actions, even when it was difficult. This understanding has helped me navigate challenges and build trust in both personal and professional relationships.

I was raised with the foundation moral standard and beliefs at an early age. Because of the experiences of life and the foundation that was already set, I really saw how God took care of me and my family. because of the challenges we had faced after my father's death. Not all situations was bad. The point that I'm making, you get to see it firsthand just by living life.

This is my point. I experienced the challenges early, but saw God's hand bringing us through each time. *"Though the waters thereof roar and be troubled, though the mountains shake with the swelling thereof."* Psalms 46:3 When I faced difficulties, it seemed like an insurmountable obstacle. However, through faith and perseverance, I found that through prayers and faith. This experience taught me the importance of prayers and faith that comes from a higher power.

Prayers is communion with God. When I'm praying , I'm talking to God and He is talking to me at the same time. A lot of times, when I commune with God, I have to wait on him. He may not answer when I want him, but he is an on time God. A lot of times, when God is answering me, His answer is no. He knows what's best for us, that's why prayer life and communion with God is very important in my life. *"To everything there is a season, and a time for every purpose under heaven: a time to be born, and a time to die; a time to plant, and a time to pluck up that which is planted".* Ecclesiastes 3: 1-8 This establishes the central theme of the passage, highlighting the distinct periods in life and the cyclical nature of events. In other words God will answer your prayers or change your circumstances just trust and believe. Now, do you want to take time to wait? Learning patience is vital. The biggest factor is fear. Fear is false evidence that appeal real. Sometimes when your back is up against a wall and you're fearful, you don't know what the outcome of a situation is going to be. We might have a tendency to react differently, but if you just wait on God and see what the end is going to be, everything will be all right. Fear can be a bad thing in a case of not patiently waiting on Him, and it's very important.

I've taken matter in my own hands and not wait on God many times I end up messing up the situation simply by not waiting. Sometimes, what bothers us is when we don't know what the end is going to be. For example in Genesis 17, *I will give Sarah a son. She will be the mother of many nations. We try to help God out just as Abraham and Sarah did. Therefore Sarah laughed within herself, saying, after I'm waxed old shall I have pleasure, my lord being old also. And the LORD said unto Abraham, Wherefore did Sarah laugh, saying Shall I of a surety bear a child, which I am old? Is anything to old hard for the LORD? At the time appointed I will return unto thee, according to the time life, and Sarah shall have a son. Then Sarah denied, saying, I laughed not; for she was afraid. And he said, Nay; but thou didst laugh.*

They wouldn't wait on God to give them a child that He promised them. Sarah went to the handmaiden Hagar and had her to conceive a child with her husband Abraham. Sarah believed that she was too old to bear a child. Therefore she and Abraham took matters in their own hand without waiting on God. The story teaches us about the consequences of taking matters into our own hands without trusting in divine timing. It highlights the importance of patience and faith, showing that when we act out of impatience, we may encounter unforeseen challenges. Ultimately, it serves as a reminder to rely on faith and trust in life's natural flow.

I was in my own state of mind doing things my way, I couldn't see the way God was seeing it. This made me question God because I was impatient on waiting on Him. Although I was taught better, I allowed my flesh to take over.

When that happened to me, I can assure you one thing that happened—I lost focus. I was taught that God will provide for me regardless of what the situation is. So when I got out of focus, I start seeing things in a carnal state of mind instead of a spiritual state of mind.

That's where I lost focus.. It was very important for me to regain my focus and maintain my spiritual thoughts, not my carnal mind. Jesus asked the question to challenge people's motives and to test their faith. Jesus asked the question multiple times in the Bible. John 11:25-26 Jesus asked Martha this question; *Do you believe this? That I am the resurrection and the life? After raising her brother Lazarus from the dead. He that believes in me, though he dead, yet shall he live Jesus said.* "People come to believe in God because they believe He has provided for their needs and circumstances. Others may find a sense of purpose and meaning in life through their faith I have heard this a fair number of times—testimonies around how people who were in challenging situations with obstacles before them, hurdles and mountains of life to climb. But God helped them through it, which is what birthed their faith in God. Do you believe that God is able to help you in whatever problem you face in your personal life? Jesus said in Mark 9:23-24, "*If thou canst believe, all things are possible to him that believeth. I believe, but help through my unbelief."* Prayer that acknowledges doubt and asks for God's help to strengthen faith. When we're unable to do it ourselves, it is a request for supernatural help to increase our faith. It is an acknowledgment of human weakness and the struggle between faith and doubt. It is a recognition of Jesus as the source, strength, and faith. It's a model of honest prayer demonstrating that God welcomes requests for help in overcoming doubt. This teaches us that doubt is not a bad thing, but a human thing. It teaches us that God is greater than our doubt. All we have to do is to trust in Him with all our heart, soul, and mind. The decisions that we make in life are important. Some choices that are made you cannot get over. It teaches us that belief in the infinite God by finite humans is an act of exploration in our lives. We need help from a higher power.

If you trust in God and have that belief, we know that all things are possible. He told us that in His word, and we have to believe that. Some things in life you really can't do alone. You need help from other people. So I would encourage you to get with people that can help you.. Their help can increase your doubt about failing or succeeding in that process because I've experienced it in my life. There are some things that I went through with starting my business that I really didn't know, but by talking to the right people, they helped me to achieve my goals to start my own business. However, by talking to the right people through networking it allowed me to connect with experienced professionals who provided valuable insights and advice. By building relationships with industry leaders, I gained access to resources and opportunities that I wouldn't have found on my own. These connections were instrumental in navigating challenges and securing partnerships that propelled my business forward.

The first piece of advice I would give is to set aside time for prayer and to read materials like this book to help. Seek out a church that can help you grow spiritually of your choice. Spiritual growth is essential for developing a deeper understanding of oneself and one's purpose in life. It provides a sense of peace and resilience in the face of challenges. Spiritual growth will teach you how to handle all situations in life.

When you do this, you are getting good Bible resources and you can grow from these lessons and that will help you in your everyday walk of life. This book is intended to help those who do not know God develop a relationship with him after reading it. It provides practical guidance on understanding biblical principles and applying them to daily life. Through thought-provoking questions and reflective exercises, readers are encouraged to deepen their faith and spiritual awareness. My book includes personal stories and testimonies that illustrate the transformative power of a strong relationship with God.

This chapter is important because of what you believe is how you behave. The question is do you believe that God can? If you don't believe, what is it that keep you from believing? Perhaps it could have been experience or something else. I'm here to witness to you that God will never forsake or leave you.

Sometimes a person may not know where they stand in their spiritual walk with God, God did not give us the spirit of fear. I'm writing this book to help you see yourself and improve your spiritual walk with God—get a closer walk with him and get a relationship with him. Not just going to church but have a personal relationship with him. This isn't going to happen overnight. This is a process, but you got to get it started this is what will help you in your walk with him.

How do you see your relationship with God. Philippians 4:13: *"I can do all things through Christ who strengthens me."* It's a well-known verse in Christianity, emphasizing that believers can overcome challenges and live a fulfilling life with Christ's power. I know for myself. I can do all things because I believe that parable because he made a promise to us that he would sustain us. With that if you make one step, he'll make two, this is a true statement.

I'm the deacon at the church. That's where I get my spiritual food from and it's been helping me for 66 years and I'm grateful to be there. We've had some tough times. I don't think everything was a bed of roses. But doing the ups and downs of life, it teaches you that even with your spiritual walk with life, there are ups and downs.

It was those teachings that helped me. There's scriptures that we read all the time. I would encourage all of us to have a song in our heart, a scripture in our heart that we can fall back on anytime. So all the time you can't call your pastor in the middle of certain situations. You have to work your way out of that. So it's very important that with my spiritual background and upbringing that I keep something with me at all times in my heart and not on paper.. It's written in my heart and it's important that we do so.

QUESTIONS

1. Do you believe that you can achieve your goals?

   _____
   _____
   _____

2. What is the obstacle in your way?

   _____
   _____
   _____

3. How can you remove the obstacle?

   _____
   _____
   _____

4. What time frame are you placing on yourself?

   _____
   _____
   _____

5. What can help you remove the obstacle?

_____

_____

_____

NOTES

www.ingramcontent.com/pod-product-compliance
Lightning Source LLC
Chambersburg PA
CBHW061803070526
44586CB00023B/2686